LIGHTNING
BOLT
BOOKS™

T0015914

Ghost Hunters

Emma Carlson-Berne

Lerner Publications ◆ Minneapolis

Lerner Publications Company
An imprint of Lerner Publishing Group, Inc.
241 First Avenue North
Minneapolis, MN 55401 USA

For reading levels and more information, look up this title at www.lernerbooks.com.

Main body text set in Billy Infant Regular. Typeface provided by SparkType.

Library of Congress Cataloging-in-Publication Data

Names: Berne, Emma Carlson, 1979- author.
Title: Ghost hunters / Emma Carlson-Berne.
Description: Minneapolis : Lerner Publications, [2024] | Series: Lightning bolt books. That's scary! | Includes bibliographical references and index. | Audience: Ages 6-9 | Audience: Grades 2-3 | Summary: "Many people believe ghosts exist. Ghost hunters are using technology to try to prove it. Readers will investigate the tricks and tools used by people hunting for ghosts around the world"—Provided by publisher.
Identifiers: LCCN 2022042933 (print) | LCCN 2022042934 (ebook) | ISBN 9781728491158 (lib. bdg.) | ISBN 9798765603291 (pbk.) | ISBN 9781728498584 (eb pdf)
Subjects: LCSH: Ghosts—Juvenile literature. | Parapsychology—Investigation—Juvenile literature.
Classification: LCC BF1461 .B425 2024 (print) | LCC BF1461 (ebook) | DDC 133.1—dc23/eng/20220930

LC record available at https://lccn.loc.gov/2022042933
LC ebook record available at https://lccn.loc.gov/2022042934

Manufactured in the United States of America
1-53046-51064-11/30/2022

Table of Contents

Searching for Ghosts

The servers at Nido's restaurant in Maryland were scared. They were sure they heard a ghost stomping up the stairs. They needed . . . ghost hunters!

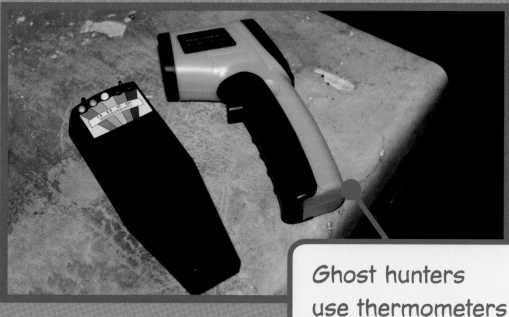

Ghost hunters use thermometers to find cold spots.

Ghost hunters carry lots of equipment to search for evidence of ghosts.

Soon a team arrived. They set up video cameras and audio recorders. The servers wanted the ghost hunters to prove the ghost existed.

Going to the Ghosts

Ghost hunters look for proof of ghosts or paranormal activity. Ghost hunters try to capture both ghostly sounds and images.

Ghost hunters use tools to find changes in electricity nearby.

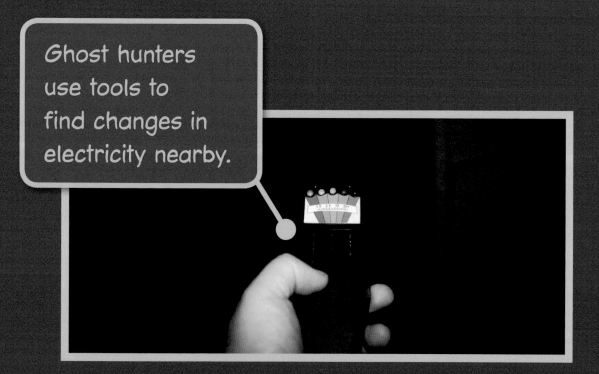

The Stanley Hotel in Colorado is said to be haunted.

People might report a haunting in their homes or businesses. The ghost hunters check it out.

Some psychics use a spirit board to talk to ghosts.

Sometimes ghost hunters learn about a haunting from a psychic. Psychics try to communicate with the ghost using their minds and voices.

Ghost hunting is usually done at night. Ghost hunters often investigate abandoned places such as old prisons, asylums, or schools.

Eastern State Penitentiary is a popular site for ghost hunters.

Ghost hunters believe that ghosts leave evidence, such as cold spots or blobs of white light called orbs.

Ghost hunters act as ghost detectives!

Sometimes ghost hunters don't see any ghosts in a haunted place until later . . . when they appear in their photos!

Some say that orbs are the spirits of people who have died. Some say they turn into orbs so that they can travel more easily.

Some paranormal investigators go to strange places to find ghosts, like military submarines!

Ghost hunters might search alone or with a small group. Some use walkie-talkies to stay in touch. Solo ghost hunters need to be careful exploring areas that could be unsafe.

If a hunter finds a ghost, they might ask if the ghost wants something. Sometimes, ghost hunters say, the ghosts answer.

Many people died trying to escape Alcatraz prison, making many people believe it is haunted.

Tools of the Trade

Ghost hunters bring equipment with them to capture proof of ghosts. Since many hauntings are said to happen at night, a night vision camera is useful.

Some ghost hunters might bring night vision goggles with them to help them quickly see something in the dark.

Night vision goggles can detect light that humans can't see on their own.

Many ghost hunters also use an electromagnetic field (EMF) reader to check for a change in electricity nearby. Ghost hunters believe spirits give off electrical signals.

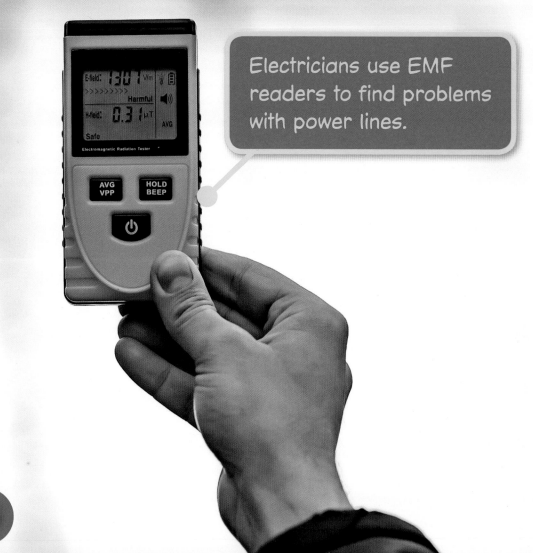

Electricians use EMF readers to find problems with power lines.

Some ghost hunters use special cameras that can see infrared light, a kind of light that humans can't see.

The EMF reader will beep when it picks up changes in electricity. Some believe these changes signal a ghost is nearby.

A voice recorder is another important ghost-hunting tool. Ghost hunters want to capture any sounds a ghost might make, such as banging, speaking, or crying.

Ghost hunters have to be careful when exploring dark or crumbling old buildings.

No one knows if ghosts really exist. Ghost hunters believe they do, though. They are ready to collect proof with their special tools. When people see or hear strange things, ghost hunters can investigate.

Ghost hunter Lorraine Warren claimed she was psychic and could speak to spirits.

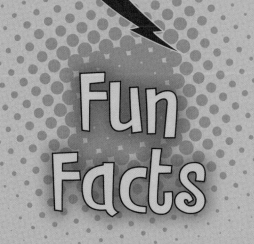

Fun Facts

- Ghost hunters use digital voice recorders to capture what they call electronic voice phenomena. They believe this is proof of ghosts speaking.

- Ghost hunters believe ghosts soak in heat from the air, so that's why they say cold spots can mean a ghost is near.

- In 2005, three ghost hunters were arrested in Salem, Massachusetts. They were so busy looking for ghosts that they didn't notice they were on private property!

Eastern State Penitentiary

Eastern State Penitentiary in Pennsylvania was one of the first prisons to use solitary confinement. The prison punished people by putting them in cells all by themselves. Ghost hunters say that the prison's abandoned halls are full of the ghosts of the unhappy prisoners. When a team of investigators visited, they said they saw a ghostly man walking through one of the cell blocks and heard voices coming from empty spots. Another team said they recorded objects moving around by themselves.

Glossary

abandoned: given up, left empty, or unused

asylum: a place for the care of the poor or the physically or mentally ill

investigate: to observe or study by close examination

night vision: the ability to see in the dark

paranormal: something that has not yet been explained by science

psychic: a person who claims to be sensitive to nonphysical or paranormal forces

Learn More

Abdo, Kenny. *Ghosts*. Minneapolis: Fly!, 2020.

Britannica Kids: Ghost
https://kids.britannica.com/kids/article/ghost/574605

Kiddle: Ghost Facts for Kids
https://kids.kiddle.co/Ghost

Ransom, Candice. *Eerie Haunted Houses*. Minneapolis: Lerner Publications, 2021.

Toronto Public Library: Are Ghosts Real?
https://kids.tpl.ca/wonders/682

Troupe, Thomas Kingsley. *Searching for Ghosts*. Mankato, MN: Black Rabbit Books, 2021.

Index

Photo Acknowledgments

Images used: Juiced Up Media/Shutterstock.com, p. 4; eddtoro/Shutterstock.com, p. 5; Juiced Up Media/Shutterstock.com, p. 6; Carol M. Highsmith Archive via the Library of Congress, p. 7; danilsnegmb/Getty Images, p. 8; Bryan Kelley/Getty Images, p. 9; Peter Kim/Shutterstock.com, p. 10; Juan Vte. Muñoz/Shutterstock.com, p. 11; Stuart Villanueva/The Galveston County Daily News/AP Images, p. 12; Marni Moore/EyeEm, p. 13; O.PASH/Shutterstock.com, p. 14; CreativeHQ/Shutterstock.com, p. 15; Olena Tatarintseva/Shutterstock.com, p. 16; Marijan Murat/picture alliance via Getty Images, p. 17; Vink Fan/Shutterstock.com, p. 18; Chris Pizzello/Invision/AP Images, p. 19.

Cover image: Alessandro Pierpaoli/shutterstock.com.